betrayal in the city

E.A.E.P. Drama Library

The original version of *Betrayal in the City* was first produced at the Kenya National Theatre in May 1975 by Mr. Tirus Gathwe with the following cast:

Doga   Kitheka Mutui
Nina   Anne Wanjugu
Jusper   Sidede Onyulo
Jere   Martin Okelo
Atema   Mhlangabezi ka-vundla
Mosese   Ayieko Aduke
Askari   Peter Leroi Oderrow
Regina   Rosemary Jommo
Wendo   Dhus Ohawa
Tumbo   Philip Chege
Kabito   J.T.N. Karegi
Mulili   Paul Onsongo
Boss   Mick Ndisho
Tom   John Mwiricha
Palace Staff   Elija Konga Mbandu, Esther Njiru, Albert Wandogo, Isaiah Shimuli, Anne Clara Wanjiru, Anne Rama, Barrett Odhiambo, Mary Adams

Characters in the play

Doga   an old man
Nina   his wife
Jusper Wendo   their son
Jere   soldier, later prisoner
Mulili   his colleague, later farmer
Askari   prison warder
Mosese   ex-lecturer, now prisoner
Regina   his sister, also Wendo's girl-friend
Tumbo   government official
Kabito   government official
Nicodemo   government official
Boss   Head of State of Kafira
Guards, palace staff and people

Time   the present

Place   Kafira (an independent African state)

Author's note
This play is best done on a composite set in order to avoid wasting much time during scence changes.

betrayal
in the city

a play by
Francis Imbuga

EAST AFRICAN EDUCATIONAL PUBLISHERS
Nairobi • Kampala • Dar es Salaam

Published by
East African Educational Publishers Ltd.
Brick Court, Mpaka Road/Woodvale Grove
Westlands, P.O. Box 45314, Nairobi

East African Educational Publishers Ltd.
P.O Box 11542, Kampala

Ujuzi Educational Publishers Ltd
P.O. Box 31647, Kijito-Nyama, Dar es Salaam

© Francis Imbuga 1976, 1987

First published by East African Educational Publishers Ltd. 1987

Reprinted 1988 (thrice), 1989, 1990 (thrice), 1997 (twice)
1999, 2000, 2001, 2002 (twice), 2003, 2004

ISBN 9966-46-360-7

Printed in Kenya by Sunlitho Ltd.
P.O. Box 13939, Nairobi

act one

scene one

Early morning. A lonely grave surrounded by dry thorny branches. A wooden bowl sits at the centre of the grave; in it, a few silver coins. When the grave is fully lit, it will be seen that a crack runs right across it. Birds, insects, frogs, etc. join in song. A drum beats, stops, beats again and stops. In the distance, a male voice laments. Now the lament fills the air as Doga enters immediately trailed by his wife, Nina, weeping silently. Slowly they move towards the grave. Suddenly the song dies on Doga's lips. He stands still, transfixed to the spot. Nina peers forward, then nervously moves back step by step; Doga turns and sees his retreating wife.

Doga   Nina, stop where you are! What sort of mother are you? Do you now fear to set eyes on this evil that has been done on your own son's grave? For hours and hours you shook with grief. For days you wailed over his still body as those who saw him die unfolded the story. Will you now tremble at the mere sight of the shadow of that evil? Come, come help me put the thorns in place before the morning grows out of our hands.

Nina   Who would have thought they would follow him even to his grave? Only the final night, yet with it the ceremony is gone.

Doga   It is now clear that the man at whose hands my son died lives among us even now. This is proof enough. What we ignored as empty talk now begins to take on grave meaning.

Nina   But where was Jusper when they did this? We
asked him to keep watch, didn't we? Where was he
when the murderers followed his brother beyond the
grave? Did they get at him?

Doga   Come, see for yourself. Smell Nina, smell.
Does not the smell of petrol penetrate your nose? Look,
it was no common earthquake that made this crack. This
is the work of a stray clansman, one who thinks he has
the strength to fight those who taught him how to hold
a spear. Thank heaven they did not get at him.

Nina   God be praised. But . . . but where is Jusper?
I do not understand why he did not shout for help when
he saw them do this to his brother's remains!

Doga   You forget the boy's illness. We were not sure
that he would stay here all night. Besides, what with last
night's downpour, they must have tried to do it while
he took shelter. When he returned, he frightened them
away.

Nina   But where is he now? Doga, my heart fails
me. This is not our day. Let us get away from this place.
We shall return when we know where Jusper is. Look, it
seems there was a struggle here.

Doga   Jusper is alright where he is.

Nina   He is our only hope. If they should harm him,
I will hang myself and raise a curse upon the whole clan.

Doga   Hope? I am surprised that you still talk of hope.
Nina, we buried our hope the day Adika was gunned
down. Come, let us not waste any more time. Get me soil.

Nina   But what do you . . . ?

Doga   Get me soil, did you hear, soil. We must fill
this crack and for a while disguise the evil that lives
among us. The ceremony must go on as planned. I do

not want the spirits of the dead to turn wild with anger on account of a ceremony unperformed.

Nina It would be wrong for us to sit on this evil. We cannot outwit our ancestors. Let us do what is expected of us. Let us send word to the sub-chief and . . . .

Doga The sub-chief! Who is the sub-chief? A mouse does not share a bowl with a cat.

Nina It is the noise he makes that I fear.

Doga The sub-chief! Who is the sub-chief? Have you so soon forgotten the rumour that now bears the same weight as noble truth? Nina, when dry thunder tears the sky before our eyes, do we forget the storm of yesterday? Women!! Women will never think beyond the beds upon which they hide for the night. The sub-chief! Did he not come from that same stomach that mothered Chagaga?

Nina Nothing we do will bring Adika back. You know how patiently we have waited for this day. A little delay will do no harm, but if we hide the truth, I fear something will go wrong.

Doga The ceremony shall go on as planned. I do not want it delayed. A cloudy sky does not always cry rain.

Nina But if they should know what has happened, they will whisper and say we ignored tradition. They will boycott my son's shaving ceremony. Please Doga, let us report this matter.

Doga Tradition condemns the shedding of a kinsman's blood. Nina, what will you teach me about tradition? Go get me soil. (*Exit Nina. Doga picks up the money from the bowl.*) Cold, cold money. Three cold silver coins. No warmth, no life. What a strange way to appease the dead. Adika, my son, do not let them deceive you with money.

When you came into this world to search for your death,
you found money here. Now you are silent, but money
is still here. Do not let them tempt you. Follow them to
the bitter end. Follow them up hills and down valleys.
(*to audience*) What is in money that is more precious than
life? Only a handful of coins cost us a son, killed in
the city. People say there were many of them, all marching
in the same manner. Suddenly, the shooting broke out.
People fled in all directions, but my son's lonely body lay
in the middle of the street. Only four bullets were fired
that day. Adika had four bullet wounds in his chest. Two
weeks after we buried him, the sub-chief's brother was
dismissed from his job. Rumour has it that he later said
that he did it in self-defence. (*prolonged laugh from off
stage*) That is the voice of the brother of the silent one.
They were our only children. When he heard of the
death of his brother, Jusper was never the same again.
He became wild at the funeral, singing songs of
vengeance; then they came and took him away. Said he
was dangerous to peace loving people and had to be
cooled down. When they brought him back after three
months, he was no longer the son we knew. (*Second
laugh, this time it's much nearer. Doga hides behind the bush
as Jusper enters, still laughing. He wears a red gown. He
suddenly stops, stares at the grave then turns to the audience.*)

   Jusper   People say I am mad. My own mother thinks
I am out of my mind. My father calls me crazy. But that,
(*points to the grave*) that when I show them will prove I have
sense here (*points to his head*). My here is powerful; that is
why Regina accepted me for a boyfriend. That is why I
know the difference between the sun, Jupiter and Jusper.
Hey, come to think of it! You and I have never seen

Jupiter, except...? Except on paper. *Jupiter!—Absent sir. Jusper!—Present sir. Justice!—Absent sir.* Yes I've got it. Jupiter and justice are one and the same. They are neither here nor there. No. That is a debatable point, a philosophical point. That is me, Jusper Wendo, Esquire, almost B.A., Kafira University. (*A bird sings.*) I like that bird for its bravery. Comes to the wrong place and doesn't even bother to keep quiet about it. Coming to this ceremony is positively criminal except for close relatives like me. (*strides to the grave*) Adika! Adika! Please come and back me up. Come help me stop mother and father from growing old. We'll need them. We'll need every available person. You know what? We have even accepted the contribution of birds. We need songs, war songs .... Adika! Adika! .... Alright you are too late. (*begins to imitate his favourite cowboy*) Brother or no brother you gonna join the struggle by force. We gotta restore human dignity, right? Wake up, man! Alright; you're rioting in your grave and you gonna pay for it. You gonna face the squad, and this time it's gonna be public. (*picks up two sticks and holds them as if they were two pistols, one in each hand*) Squad, attention! Aim! ..... one, two, three, two, one, fire! Tutututututututu! Squad, at ease! Hey, sergeant, why you lookin' sad eeh? He ya brother or somethin'? Don' worry, don' worry. You were servin' your bloody nation, right? (*Enter Nina with soil.*)

Nina   Jusper, where were you?

Jusper   Serving the nation.

Nina   How could you desert your brother!?

Jusper   It was an order.

Nina   What order? You take off that thing and go and put on something decent. The others will soon be here.

Jusper Is Regina with them?

Nina Perhaps.

Jusper Girlfriend Number One; she ought to come.

Nina She's far away in the city. Where is your father?

Doga (*whispering rather loudly*) Do not detain him. Let him go.

Jusper He can't go; he is dead.

Nina My son, please go and put on a clean shirt.

Jusper A clean shirt? No. Not after the murder.

Nina What shall we do now? The illness creeps back on him. Jusper, do you know what day today is?

Doga Don't remind him.

Jusper Come and see for yourself. (*points at the crack*) Do you see this river, all this water? I threw him in there. Don't tell me he swam away, because he didn't. He was dead when I threw him there.

Nina He thinks he has killed you. Please do something before he spoils the ceremony.

Doga I told you to shut that mouth!

Jusper Alright, I will shut up. Nobody need know I am a murderer. (*throws the sticks away*) After all, it was great fun. Now I know how they feel when they do it. Shall I go and confess I did it?

Nina Yes my son, go and put on a clean shirt and then you can confess.

Jusper Do you think they will harm me if I address the rally?

Nina No, they won't. Just go and put on your shirt first.

Jusper Will they put him in a government coffin, do you think?

Nina   Good God! What shall we do?

Jusper   I will go and recommend a government coffin with many handles so that everybody will help lower him into the grave. (*He smiles, stands at attention, salutes, then exits, military style.*)

Nina   He has never behaved like this before.

Doga   His eyes were full of sleep.

Nina   Why did he think he had killed you?

Doga   It was his brother he thought he had killed. I saw him address the grave as if Adika sat right on top of it. It was both strange and frightening.

Nina   I hope he will be calm at the ceremony. What shall we do if he grows wild? We can't lock him up during his brother's ceremony, can we?

Doga   It is his fate. They locked him up during the burial.

Nina   Come, let us put this day in God's hands. The drummers will soon be here. (*They kneel in front of the grave and sing.*)

> *When we walk with the Lord*
> *In the light of his way*
> *What a glory he sheds on our way*
> *When we do his good will*
> *He abides with us still*
> *Unto all who will trust and obey*
>
>> *Trust and obey*
>> *For there is no other way*
>> *To be happy in Jesus*
>> *But to trust and obey*

Nina   (*praying*) Father, Maker of all that crawl and all that fly, we are dry of words, but we put this day in your

hands. We ask this through Jesus Christ our Saviour,
Amen. (*Jere and Mulili enter, the latter carries a bottle of
beer, from which he will drink every now and then.*)

Jere   Old people, you waste your time. There is to be
no ceremony.

Doga   Is it to us you speak?

Mulili   No ceremony! That the final.

Doga   A shaving ceremony is no child's play.

Mulili   Who you call child, eeh? Jere, you tell him.
Tell him what I does with stubbon old mens.

Jere   The ceremony is cancelled in the interest of
peace.

Doga   In the interest of peace? Whose peace?

Mulili   We wants no anymore bloody bloodshed. We
have seen enough. Just who you wants to murder next?

Doga   Murder? Me? Young man, have you nothing
to do with your time that you come and throw your
weight about the grave of an innocent harmless dead?
And you young man, is this a time to laugh?

Jere   We are on duty. We serve the nation.

Mulili   Repeat to them Jere, repeat. Tell them this
grave no longer belong them.

Nina   You took our all, but you will not take the
grave from us. If you do not go now, I shall strip and
show you the poor naked bones you have left me. Do
you want to be blinded by the nakedness of your
grandmother's agemate?

Jere   No, we do not ask for blindness. You see, this
friend of mine does not belong here. He doesn't know
our ways.

Doga   Then he should keep quiet instead of turning
our hearts over and over.

Mulili Big coward. Why you doesn't let her get on with it. How many naked body I have seen and I am still Mulili with my two eyes, natural? Look, no glass goggles.

Doga Let us forget he ever was born. Young man, the shape of your head even with that thing on is a familiar shape. Tell me, are you not Kaleka's son?

Jere I am.

Doga Then listen to me. Your father and I shared the same knife at circumcision. What devil makes you look me in the face?

Jere I do not look you in the face. I know the bitterness in your heart.

Mulili Big coward. Jere, you a woman! (*They stare at him briefly.*)

Jere Old man, if I had the power, I would let you go on. I would even take part in the ceremony. I knew Adika well.

Doga Do you know that even as we stand here, a stranger who hardly knew him lies in prison because of him?

Mulili That no matter. He go against law and order. Tell us new thing or make clear out of here. You are tresspasser.

Doga Empty words will be your downfall. May you die the way Adika did!

Mulili Hey Jere, did you heard that? You tell him me I am man with action, not words. Come on tell . . . .

Jere Shut up! (*silence, then Mulili chuckles softly*) Old man, do as I tell you for the moment. It's safer. Look, this is the signed order.

Nina Do not show us letters when you know well what you did to our eyes. You have blinded us, left us in

darkness, and then as if that is not enough, you show us
letters. Look young man, that is where our eyes are—
under that mound.

Mulili Your people full of primitive. Instead going
to find how the other is, they comes and get stuck with
dead one.

Doga What other one?

Mulili You see now, he now being pretend. All
they wants is the bloody ceremony.

Doga Kaleka's son, what is it he talks about? What
pretence does he mean?

Jere He talks of Jusper.

Doga What about Jusper?

Jere I can't believe it. I can't believe you are in the
dark.

Nina What has Jusper done?

Jere Have you seen him at all since last night?

Nina Yes, he was even here this morning. We asked
him to guard the grave last night, but when we arrived
this morning, he was not here; then after a little while,
he came. See what they did while he was away! (*Jere
inspects the grave.*)

Jere My God, I can't believe it.

Mulili What have happen? Have the guard eat the
body? (*laughs loudly*)

Jere Be serious for once you devil.

Mulili I am professional soldier by profession.

Jere I didn't believe the rumour. It is good he is
dead.

Doga Who?

Jere Chagaga.

Nina The sub-chief's brother?

Jere Yes. (*pause*) Jusper killed him.

Doga
Nina } Jusper?

Jere Yes, last night.

Nina This is a trick!

Jere It is no trick. People saw him drag the body to the river, and when they sent a search team there, they sure enough found the body.

Nina This is a trick!

Jere He even confessed it himself.

Doga Confessed? When?

Jere A few minutes before they sent us here. He came dressed in a white shirt and confessed. Beat his chest in front of all the people and said he had done it. At first people ran away from him, as if he suffered from some horrible infectious disease. After a while, they picked up stones and started to stone him. The whole crowd was throwing stones. When he fell down, the people took to their heels, thinking him dead.

Doga He is not dead then?

Jere No.

Doga Where is he now?

Mulili All small murderers get arrest.

Jere They took him away and asked us to come and guard the grave.

Nina It was all my fault. I sent him to them. I assured him that they would not harm him. I wish I knew what rally he said he wanted to address.

Mulili You see. I says these too be murderers.

Doga If Jusper killed Chagaga, then he is not mad. We lack a name for his illness. But days have changed.

Kaleka's son, I have nothing else to offer you;
(*handing him a pocket Bible*) take this. May God
open your eyes to the suffering of your people. Nina,
tears are for the young, our own wells are dry. Come,
let us go away. (*Doga and Nina leave.*)

Jere   (*after long silence*) You disgust me. I know you
are Boss's cousin but still you disgust me. How
could you possibly speak like that to those two poor
creatures?

Mulili   You want me sing to them, eeh? Chicken
heart, that is what you be. Sometimes I ask myself why
you possession that thing between your legs.

Jere   It took a stranger for the truth to come to the
surface. A stranger to the clan, like you. That man is still
in prison even now. Mulili, if you still have even the
smallest part of your original human heart, let us allow
these people to carry on with the ceremony.

Mulili   What!?

Jere   Boss will not know it. No one need know.

Mulili   My future depend on this. If I keep law and
order, a big farmer I become when I retired. Boss
promise me that and you know. . . I be his eye and his ear
here. I say no ceremony.

Jere   The ceremony is on.

Mulili   Me count out. I doesn't want to lost that
farm. Boss promise many acre of farm and grade cattles.
I doesn't want to lost it because for primitive ceremony.

Jere   I looked in that old woman's eyes and I saw the
futility of calling ourselves citizens of Kafira. We must
allow them even if it's against the law. . . . I am sure there
will be no trouble. After all, you and I will be on
stand-by.

Mulili   Duty be duty and we on duty now. We must do what expected of us.

Jere   Even if it means killing a friend?

Mulili   These you call friend?

Jere   Then I did wrong. I let you get away with it. I saved you.

Mulili   Who, me you saved? How? When?

Jere   When you let Mustafa escape, did I open my mouth? Why should we not allow these two to perform a harmless ceremony for their dead in that same spirit?

Mulili   Mustafa's case be different. Nobody likely to know he go across border.

Jere   Will you help me?

Mulili   No. Not this. It too dangerous.

Jere   Then I'll do it alone. I shall go to the village and announce that the ceremony is on.

Mulili   You jokes. You expects me to quiet about it?

Jere   No I don't, but I will go on. These are my people. They have done no wrong. Look at the grave. This is proof that their son was murdered. The man wanted to rid himself of the ghost by burning the body.

Mulili   You still believes in ghost?

Jere   (*losing his temper*) Put that bottle down and listen to me. That boy there died for Kafira's progress. He was slaughtered like a goat and sacrificed for a non-existent peace and harmony. Surely he deserves this ceremony!

Mulili   The fellow should ought have know best than incite his fellow students to rioting. They should ought have follow proper channels.

Jere   What do you know about proper channels?

Mulili   This, that even although majority lecturers at Kafira University be expatriate, that not his business.

He go there to learn, not criticise policy that he know
nothing about.

Jere   Do you know they only acted referees in a
match between our own sides? It was an empty battle
where we fought against ourselves.

Mulili   Who say that? Who say we fight each
against ourself? They cross the river, go the other side
and call themself interllectual. They hurl abuse at our
symbol of national securicor. A lot public fund and time
go be wasted in bring the situation back to normal.
They were retard progress, not for progress.

Jere   I refuse to kneel down for theoretical
progress.

Mulili   Then become student now. (*He looks at
Jere, goes to the grave, scoops some soil and lets it fall between his
fingers.*) Dust to dust, ash to . . . .

Jere   Will you shut up you heartless brute!

Mulili   Brute? Where you get that from?

Jere   Get out of my sight! (*aims a pistol at him*)

Mulili   (*hands up*) Alright, I am sorrowful. I honest
doesn't know it will affect you.

Jere   Get out of my sight now! (*Mulili begins to walk
off. Jere shoots as Mulili dives off stage.*)

Mulili   Hey you, what you thinks you do?! You shall
pays for it!

Jere   Go shoot your mouth wherever you will.
(*Jere goes to the grave, takes a coin from his pocket and drops
it into the bowl. He kneels down and bends over the grave
in prayer. Lights fade out slowly.*)

scene two

A prison cell equipped with the usual prison stuff:
pail, mat, blanket, etc. At one of the corners,
Mosese sits with his back to the audience. Suddenly, the door
is opened and Jere pushed in. He falls just short of
Mosese, but the latter is unmoved.

Jere   My friend, why . . . . .

Askari   Next time you call me your friend, you will
lose a tooth. What makes me think I am a better man
than you!? Do you think I live off answering such
foolish questions? You are inside, I am out, now if that
doesn't make sense to you, something else will.

Jere   A lot of things don't make sense to me, you
included.

Askari   My God, this is the wrong place for you.
The place for lunatics is three doors down the corridor.

Jere   You mean three doors up the corridor?

Askari   That could land you into more trouble.
Three doors up the corridor is the office of the head of
this institution.

Jere   Is he in or out?

Askari   In, and he won't be much use to you when
I start educating you.

Jere   Has it ever occurred to you that the outside of
this cell may well be the inside of another?

Askari   (*looking around to make quite sure that no
mistake has been made*) Look, people don't question
things here. You make your own life more unbearable.

Jere   I know, but do you know chameleons?

Askari   I have had enough of you and your chameleons.

Jere   They are masters of environmental adaptation.

Askari   You waste your time. Now I see why you tried to make yourself champion of justice, bleeding meaningless words.

Jere   My experience during the last few weeks has made it necessary that I talk. It is as if I have been born again. I have never felt so confident in my life.

Askari   That is why you are best ignored. Here I am wasting time talking to you instead of helping the others to fill in forms for your rehabilitation.

Jere   Rehabilitation? After only two days?

Askari   Yes; you will need it. It's the only way out of here, otherwise you will never be allowed to mix freely. You see, we have research stations dotted all over the countryside. Experiments at these research stations show that rehabilitation is invaluable for all who pass through here. You should be thankful that in spite of your contribution to the national headache, we still give your future some consideration.

Jere   I am truly grateful now that I know what awaits me. I didn't know you took such pains.

Askari   Experts had to be imported to give meaning to the data. It wasn't the type of work any of these local pretenders would handle.

Jere   I see your point. No previous experience, eeh?

Askari   Don't cut me short. You do the listening, I talk.

Jere   You work like the meteorological department. No public questions into methods used, and no assurance.

Askari   I can see you have come to stay. What has the meteorological department got to do with what goes on here?

Jere   They advise people to spread their blankets out, then unexpected rain falls from the seemingly clear sky. By then, it is too late to fetch umbrellas. (*silence*) Who is he?

Askari   A more sensible man than you. Used to be a drug addict though. Hey, you! What do you think you're doing showing us your back?

Mosese   I have no front.

Jere   Dead right. Shake my five, shake my five.

Askari   Shut up! You, can't you talk?

Mosese   It is prudent to be silent. But it doesn't prove I am dumb.

Jere   Dead right once more. It's amazing the people you bring here.

Mosese   I said everything in mitigation. All I had to say, but it did not help. Words have lost meaning to me. Rehabilitation, nationalisation, africanisation. What do all these words mean? What is africanisation in your mother tongue?

Askari   (*visibly embarrassed*) I—I don't answer such foolish questions. You answer him. What is africanisation in your mother tongue?

Jere   Do you and I share a mother tongue?

Askari   Correct! Now don't you ask any other foolish questions. I am here to see that you ask no questions.

Mosese   Then why were you so uneasy when I was silent a little while ago? Why do you now stop me from asking questions?

Jere   It's a perfect example of what goes on outside. No one is sure of what should be done.

Askari   You are wrong. Our assessment has never

been wrong. Take this fellow, for example. When they brought him in last night, he was all questions. We calculated that two mature strokes would ease the tension. It worked perfectly. This is where the research stations come in. You see, like all liquids have different boiling points—incidentally I did pure physics up to and including 'O' level—like all liquids have different boiling points, human beings have different breaking points. At your trial, there was enough evidence that your breaking point would be just before the end of your present jail term.

Mosese   At least you are honest.

Askari   Your friend here is two years weaker than you. Congratulations!

Mosese   Thank you. (*silence*) Sometimes I wonder why a man of your understanding should have accepted this job. I honestly think you are in the wrong place.

Askari   Many prisoners say that to me, but that is just because they don't understand Kafira. If they did, a lot of them would not be prisoners. It doesn't pay to have a hot mouth. Perhaps you were right when you said silence is the best ship home, only you realised it too late. It is now common knowledge that you are a great talker. If you decide to be silent, you will have to explain what it is you are keeping quiet about. That is how prisons work. You have to show a kind of consistency of character at the same time as you show a marked improvement.

Mosese   In that case, there can be no hope.

Askari   There is. Think about what I told you last night. It is the chance of your life. You can't afford to stick to your principles. No. Not here. That is what I told that student from the mental hospital. He took my advice and will be discharged tomorrow.

Mosese Do you mean the boy whose brother was killed?

Askari Yes; he has recovered, but he has nothing to go back to. His parents were found dead in their hut.

Mosese His parents dead?

Askari Yes, dead. Perhaps that is why he has been pardoned.

Mosese Will you do me a favour?

Askari What?

Mosese Ask him to see me before he leaves. I have a message for him to take to my sister.

Askari Tell your sister to be careful. That boy's head will never be straight.

Mosese I like the boy. He is very like his brother, and like me.

Askari Think about last night's suggestion. It's the only way I can help you. That way you will see I am not blind to these things.

Mosese I can't see myself doing it.

Askari All the same, think about it. I am not asking for an answer now. And don't listen to this fool. He will poison your mind. (*He turns to go.*)

Jere Hey you, please return my book. The senior officer said I could keep it.

Askari The senior officer said so, did he? Tell him I said no. We do not want any more trouble from you. (*exit*)

Mosese You came with books?

Jere Only one book.

Mosese   A novel?

Jere   No.

Mosese   A play?

Jere   No. A bible. The New Testament. You see,
I am a religious man.

Mosese   You?

Jere   Yes. I am a believer. I believe in travelling
light. That is why I carried the book.

Mosese   The Bible is a curious thing to deny
someone. Why did they do it?

Jere   You see, we were two men in the cell. Two
strangers. We were very bored just sitting there and
looking at each other, so we decided to do it, just to
pass time.

Mosese   Don't tell me you bent so low.

Jere   You draw conclusions too soon.

Mosese   That is what prison does to a man, but I
wasn't always like this. There were times in my past
when I never drew conclusions. There were indeed times
when I never fetched my umbrella at the sight of clouds,
however dark. Now that is only a thing of the past.

Jere   Yes, a thing of the past, like the game of last
night. Do you remember Pilate?

Mosese   Pilate? Yes, Pilate is supposed to have
humiliated Jesus.

Jere   Yes, he caned Jesus on the buttocks. Not
many of us come by such an opportunity.

Mosese   Opportunity?

Jere   Yes, opportunity. The opportunity of stripping
a king and caning his buttocks. In a way it is a pity that
it had to be Pilate. Can you imagine the sense it would
have made if only a common man had done the caning?

Mosese   I am not with you.

Jere   No? It would have been positive. As positive
as when a sick right eye is plucked out lest it infects the
left one.

Mosese   You seem to be quite at home with the
Bible.

Jere   Yes I am. I taught religious knowledge for three
years before I was drafted into the army.

Mosese   You are a soldier?

Jere   I was until I came face to face with reality.
They sent me to my own sub-location to restore peace
and order. It took me only two days to change my mind.
My friend, there is fire outside.

Mosese   That is not new. That fire has always been
there. Ever since the take-over. Mind you, things were
worse before.

Jere   I thought hard before I made up my mind.
Then I said to myself, if they take you in, carry a bible
with you. It might restore your faith in humanity. It
hasn't. You need first hand experience. You need to live
the lives of those you fight for. That is why it is
important not only to read that Pilate story, but to live it.
Only then can you understand that situation and link it
with ours. Perhaps that is why it was strangely fulfilling
acting Pilate in a cell.

Mosese   Is that why they took the book from you?

Jere   Yes. My co-actor cried out. I wonder he had
the guts to go against the law. He was Jesus and I
Pilate. That was unfortunate casting. I had wanted to
be Christ but he would not hear of it. When it came to
the caning, he couldn't stand it. He wailed like a woman
in a death home. When the guards came, I tried to

explain to them that I was only faithfully following the
script but they didn't believe me. They stripped me
naked, caned me and took the book away. That, to
them, was an eye for and eye, a tooth for a tooth; but
then they were wrong. They should have let him do it.
(*silence*) Strange. I think you and I will get on well
together. Fancy me talking to you, telling you all these
things without even knowing who you are. I am Jere
Kaleka.

Mosese   I am Mosese wa Tonga.

Jere   Mosese wa Tonga? Why did you take on a
name like that? Oh, I am sorry. I am glad to meet you.

Mosese   Me too. (*They shake hands.*)

Jere   It's a curious name, Mosese wa Tonga.

Mosese   I know. It means "remember the past".
I took it the day after I was arrested. A strange way to
be loyal. Do you remember the great row over the
changing of names?

Jere   Only vaguely.

Mosese   Blows were exchanged in the planning
committee over whether the changing of names should
be item number one or three in the development plan.
Boss had just changed his name; hence the anxiety of
some members to put it top. I changed mine for
different reasons. I had no choice but to change it.

Jere   How is that?

Mosese   You see, the day before they arrested me, I
attended a funeral. One of my students had been
murdered in cold blood. His brother has been here but
he is to be discharged tomorrow.

Jere   Is he the one the askari was talking about?

Mosese   Yes.

Jere I see. I think I . . . .

Mosese You think what?

Jere Never mind.

Mosese I have never seen anything like it before. The atmosphere was tense at the funeral. I thought for once that things would change in Kafira. But during the speeches, I learned the bitter truth. Kafira wasn't going to change after all. No. Not because of the death of one small student. A handful of politicians tried to turn the funeral service into a political rally. The service must not take more than ten minutes. The coffin should not be carried by students. Weeping in public is illegal for the academic staff. I couldn't bear it, so I told them my mind. The following day they came for me.

Jere What did they charge you with? Weeping in public?

Mosese No. Being in possession of an illegal drug. One kilogramme of opium. When they searched my car, they sure enough found the drug. I laughed. I had heard similar stories, but I never thought it would ever happen to me. The man who planted it on me was called Nicodemus. Nicodemus was my name too, but I dropped it the following day.

Jere I would have done the same. (*silence*) You have been in for the last one year, haven't you?

Mosese Yes. How did you know?

Jere I have heard about you. I also know your sister.

Mosese Who — Regina?

Jere Yes. Does she visit you?

Mosese She comes twice a month. They won't allow her to come more often.

Jere She must find it hard going without you.

Mosese   She is too soft for a prisoner's sister. Too
soft. I saw it in her eyes when she came yesterday. I saw
betrayal in her eyes. Stood in front of me and said she
wanted to go and plead for my release. I nearly slapped
her. What weakness!

Jere   Perhaps she knows you stand a chance. Is that
why the askari said there is some hope for you?

Mosese   No. That is different and more ridiculous.
They would have me clown on stage before I am
released. And that isn't a certainty either.

Jere   Clown on stage? Whatever for?

Mosese   A certain head of state is due to visit Kafira
in a few weeks' time. Now, because of his love for the
dramatic, Boss has decided that a play be performed for
the visiting head of state as part of his entertainment.
The ludicrous part of it all is that he wants the play to
be acted by prisoners. (*laughs*)

Jere   That's not funny. Why?

Mosese   It would symbolize national unity. That
would show prisoners actively involved in
nation-building.

Jere   What then has that to do with your release?

Mosese   If the exercise is a success, he has promised
the release of six hundred prisoners.

Jere   I see. In that case I feel we should volunteer
even if we won't be released.

Mosese   I will not bend so low.

Jere   I don't see it as bending low. To me, that is
sacrificing one's dignity in order to rescue others from
inevitable misery. Just think of those six hundred
families that will be re-united.

Mosese   I cannot do it. Among my friends, that

would be equivalent to kneeling in front of Boss and
pleading for mercy. Same thing as my sister wanted to
do. That would imply guilt, and I am not guilty of
anything. (*enter askari with a mug of tea*)

Askari Here, tea with milk, yet you don't even
belong to my tribe. You need a tall relative to get
anything these days. And you, because you think I am
junior officer, you can feed on your saliva. Do you know
what we call it?

Jere Tea with milk.

Askari Nonsense. The term is selective breeding
of . . .

Jere Progressive layers of humanity. It prevents an
epidemic of breaking points.

Askari Unless you are careful, I will recommend
that you be shifted to that other cell. I don't believe they
are any crazier than you are. (*sound of whistle; Askari
rushes off.*)

Jere What was that for?

Mosese Trouble in one of the cells. Here, take a sip
before he returns.

Jere Thank you. It's the only way to beat selective
breeding, by being firmly united against it.

Mosese That is why I don't believe in such crap as
the last shall be first, and blessed are the poor for they
shall inherit the kingdom of heaven! For years we
waited for the Kingdom, then they said it had come.
Our Kingdom had come at last, but no. It was all an
illusion. How many of us have set eyes upon that
Kingdom? What colour is it?

Jere I wouldn't know, but I guess it's blood red.

Mosese It was better while we waited. Now we

have nothing to look forward to. We have killed our
past and are busy killing the future. Sometimes I sit here
and look far into the past. There I see my mother
slaughtering the biggest family cock. Once every year
she slaughtered a senior cock to mark the birth of Christ.
Our children will never have such memories. Now
there is blood everywhere. Cocks are slaughtered any
day, many times a week.

Jere   Things will change.

Mosese   Perhaps. That is why I prefer to wait and
see. I will stay here and remain loyal to my principles.

Jere   Change will never come that way. You have
to make up your mind to take part in that play. That
way you will have an opportunity to meet face to face
with Boss. That way, you will have given him something
to feel ashamed of.

Mosese   You talk like that askari. He sees me silent
and thinks I am about to break, but he is wrong. He
doesn't realize that silence is a weapon just like any
other. I don't have to give legal public lectures to reveal
what it is I sit on. We all know what should be done,
but we dare not talk beyond whispers. We are dictators
of ourselves. Buying my release by acting in front of a
visiting head of state would be to betray our cause.
Why do people sit and watch in silence as the disease
spreads deep inside? I will never forgive them. They
watched in silence as soldiers beat up my innocent
sister, forcing her to give evidence against me.

Jere   You mean they . . . .

Mosese   Brutes! Murderers! Beat up my innocent
sister until she lost hearing in one ear. Why beat a
woman? Why didn't they beat me?

Jere I am sorry.

Mosese What did you say? What did I hear you say? Now, listen you! I hate people who say that to me! I hate people who sympathise with me!

Jere You need some rest. (*Mosese goes to a bundle of rags and lies down. He is still shaking with rage. Jere puts a blanket over him as Askari enters.*)

Askari What was that noise? Fighting again? You senseless brute! You were in the other cell and there was trouble. Now you are here and there is more trouble. Do you know I have seen people hang for less serious offences?

Jere I know. Innocence can be an offence.

Askari Next time you cause trouble here, you won't know when I climb on you.

Jere Leave us alone. You don't understand our language.

Askari Rioting in a public cell is not a language. I give you just one more chance. If you cause any more . . .

Jere There is no trouble here. If you want to come face to face with trouble, look out there, not here. It's out there where selective breeding blossoms

Askari You are not fit to live above the ground, you mole! And just in case you didn't know, I have once killed a man in this very cell.

Jere Congratulations! How did you manage?

Askari I am now more convinced that you are insane. Give me that mug and sleep. (*Jere hands mug to him.*) Thank you, and remember what I have just told you. Don't disturb him. (*He turns and goes off. Jere begins to organise where to sleep. Suddenly Mosese utters a terrible*

war-cry. He wriggles violently as if in a fight and then stops
suddenly. Now he stands up slowly as if in a slow motion
picture. His eyes are wide open and unblinking. He walks
round the cell greeting old friends and relatives. Jere, now
frightened, edges against the wall. At some stage, they are so
close to each other that when Mosese stretches his hand, Jere has
no alternative but to shake it.)

Mosese   Yes I was. All of us were scared that it
would go on and on. Pardon? . . . . No, I have no
immediate plans . . . . . Well, yes, I guess I will take up
this job they are offering me. . . . . . . It is my conviction
that the majority will have to go. No point in hiding
what has got to be . . . . . Yes, in the hands of the
people . . . . . Exactly, you've put it better than I could
ever have . . . . . That is a difficult one. Let's just say
I got a certain amount of satisfaction from it. You see
there is a kind of satisfaction you get out of knowing
that you are honest with yourself and with the people . . .
No, I don't exactly mean that. I would find it
difficult to take pride in what I had not helped to build.
Of course I am referring to those things we could have
done ourselves. Yes, yes.

Jere   Mosese, are you sick?

Mosese   Yes, that is why I am accepting the post . . .
No, I will forgive, but I will always remember that I
forgave them.

Jere   Mosese, can you hear me?

Mosese   I don't know about that. I suppose I will
marry, yes. . . . That was inevitable. In such a struggle,
sacrifice is necessary. Thank you; I am glad you think
so. . . . I wonder if you would have said the same thing
last evening? . . . . . Yes, thank you. See you at the

celebrations. (*He shakes a few hands and waves to well-wishers, then enters a car; quietly goes back, lies down and covers himself as before. Jere tip-toes to where Mosese now lies, bends over him for a moment, then slowly moves down stage and looks intensely at the audience.*)

Jere   When the madness of an entire nation disturbs a solitary mind, it is not enough to say the man is mad. (*fade lights*)

scene three

A small room with main and kitchen doors. A bed is neatly spread along the back wall. By the left wall is a clothes stand on which a woman's clothes hang. Regina enters by kitchen door, soap and towel in hand. She puts the two away and proceeds to wear shoes. Jusper enters by main door and tip-toes towards Regina. He wears his red academic gown.

Jusper Tutututututututu? (*Regina screams as Jusper laughs.*)

Regina I have a mind to spit in your face. How dare you do that to me?

Jusper That is hardly a way to welcome a boy-friend Regina?! It's happening everywhere, you know. They come quietly when you are least expecting them and before you realize it, they have pounced on you like hungry leopards. It's happening everywhere. It happened at my brother's grave too, only this time I was a trifle quicker. Now, don't look at me with those worried eyes. I only wanted to see what you would do if it happened to you.

Regina Next time, knock! And you better take off that thing. It makes you look more dangerous than you really are.

Jusper More mad you mean? Regina, look at me. Look at my eyes. Do you see madness in them?

Regina Sit down and have some rest.

Jusper What do you see in my eyes? (*silence*) Regina, don't be like the others. Don't try to kill me. You and your brother are the only people I have in the world, but Mosese is in; that leaves you—you alone—to build or destroy me.

Regina   You need rest.

Jusper   I don't. I will never have rest. How can I ever rest with the death of my entire family on my mind? Those brutes murdered my parents in exchange for my release. Gave me good treatment knowing well that I had nothing else to lean on except my student status. I will get my revenge some day, even if it means going it alone.

Regina   Jusper, you promised. You promised to be a good boy. Do you now talk of revenge? Remember what my brother told you before you left prison. What did he say? What did he tell you to do?

Jusper   To close my eyes, block my ears and pretend that nothing is happening. But he was wrong. Madmen don't pretend. Regina, don't take sides with them. They only use us as scapegoats, a kind of outlet for their anger. It's a shame.

Regina   It's a shame to wear that thing in the streets, and worse to have it on under my humble roof. Don't they teach you manners at that university?

Jusper   I am a philosophy student, not a student of manners. Regina, the street disease has caught up with you. You have lost your fighting spirit like everyone else in the street. As we marched up and down, some of them even shouted abusive words at us. Beggars leaning on street walls told us we were wasting time.

Regina   They were right; you waste your time.

Jusper   It is a year ago since we lost more than time. All the students want is his photograph printed in the local newspapers. We are prepared to pay for it.

Regina   You cannot force them.

Jusper   That is the tragedy of it all. We can't force

the freedom of the press to favour us. Just a photograph with the word *THANKS* above it; that's all we want.

Regina   What would you achieve by that?

Jusper   Nothing, but it is what is done in the circumstances. Why should he be an exception?

Regina   Jusper, no good will come out of this struggle. Like you, I only have two close friends left in this world. You and my brother, but my brother is inside. If anything should go wrong, we'll all be wiped out. What then is the use of this raving? Those beggars who abused you were right. They know better than to fight stones. If your brother had kept his mouth shut, he would be with us now, and if my brother had also kept quiet, he would not be wasting away in a dungeon.

Jusper   Adika died for the truth. We will not let him down. He was killed for asking whether or not we were on the right train.

Regina   At that time the important thing was not whether or not we were on the right train. No. The important thing was that at least we were on a train.

Jusper   Little knowledge is truly dangerous. I wish you knew what dreams I go through at night. I defended his remains like a man, and yet Adika won't give me a night's peace. Keeps appearing to me, and last night he nearly hit me with an enormous slide rule for shaking hands with our local sub-chief. He made me promise an impossibility.

Regina   Why don't you simply go placidly amid the noise and haste and remember what peace there may be in silence.

Jusper   You will need to be more original than that. You got that from a book.

Regina What if I did? It means something to me.
Consoles me, tells me that one day my brother will be
free again. But when you put on that thing and move up
and down the streets, I think of nothing but trouble.
Every time you wear that thing in the streets, people
think it was right for Mosese to be locked in.

Jusper It doesn't matter what the masses think if
they have no voice. That is why Adika had to go. That is
why Mosese and Jere are in: because they tried to
provide voices for the masses. They are all strong men.

Regina What is strength in a world such as ours?
What did they stand to gain by shouting louder than the
rest? Nothing. They simply put a lock to their past.

Jusper They are all heroes.

Regina Everywhere the world is full of heroism;
did they have to ride in a storm to achieve it?

Jusper We were right from the start and Mosese
knew it. They were foolish to allow him to speak,
knowing well what he would say. That is why they were
embarrassed to the extent of planting drugs on him. It
was the only way they could get him.

Regina I wish there was truth in the rumour!

Jusper What rumour?

Regina The state visit may be on after all.

Jusper So what? What difference does it make to
you? If he comes, he will only be looking for
employment.

Regina Who, him?

Jusper Yes. With so many of his subjects
unemployed, he is virtually jobless himself. He comes on
a survey mission.

Regina What's that?

Jusper   There are still many pockets in Kafira that need development, and of course we don't have the necessary man-power. Can't you see he is on a do-it-yourself kind of mission?

Regina   But if the rumour is true?

Jusper   Everybody will have three days' holiday.

Regina   Prisoners will be released to mark the occasion. Mosese may . . .

Jusper   Shit! God, what crap! Is your toilet repaired?

Regina   Yes, but wait. (*gets a toilet roll from under the bed and holds it out to him*)

Jusper   Thank you; it's a short call. (*Exit Jusper. Regina picks up a letter from the table and runs through it before Jusper returns.*)

Regina   Are you happy now?

Jusper   Nothing to be happy about a simple biological function. So it will take a state visitor to release political prisoners here in Kafira? What an act of clemency! Where is that from?

Regina   From Mr. Tumbo, my landlord. He gave me the tip.

Jusper   Let's have a look. (*takes the letter*) What does he mean?

Regina   I don't read literature. You read between the paragraphs.

Jusper   I can't trace any paragraphs here. Do you think he means it?

Regina   He does. Says he will be in charge of the whole thing himself. And don't forget he is Boss's right-hand man.

Jusper   How exactly does he hope to go about it?

Regina   That is his business, not ours.

Jusper   Why hasn't he come then? (*looks at his watch*) He is already thirty minutes late.

Regina   You know well that Tumbo is a busy man.

Jusper   What in the first place does he hope to gain by helping you? Are you sure this is not a trick—some sort of trap?

Regina   I approached him myself and asked him to speak to Boss on my behalf. That is when he told me of these other plans.

Jusper   Does he know me?

Regina   Who are you?

Jusper   I may be a student—a nobody—but at least I have a good head. This man may be tricking you. There must be something they want to know. Alright, I intend to beat him at his own game.

Regina   He won't give you a chance. He has no time to waste on students. (*There is a knock at the door. Regina, hand on lips, runs into the kitchen. Knock.*)

Jusper   Come in. (*Enter Tumbo. He is fat and somewhat overconfident, at least in this house. He wears a neat three-piece suit.*)

Tumbo   Good morning young man!

Jusper   Good morning sir!

Tumbo   Am I in the wrong place? I hope not!

Jusper   It depends on your destination.

Tumbo   Let's put it another way. Are you in the right place?

Jusper   As you can see, I am quite comfortable.

Tumbo   I notice you are one of them.

Jusper   Who?

Tumbo   The red guards.

Jusper   Red guards?

Tumbo   Yes. Red guards is my name for rioting university students. When will you learn to concentrate on what you went there for? Marching up and down the streets chanting a dead student's name will never improve things in Kafira. Never!

Jusper   That dead student was too close to me to be discussed by your kind. Whom did you want to see? My cousin?

Tumbo   Is she your cousin? Well, I should have guessed; you quite resemble each other. Is she in?

Jusper   Yes. Shall I call her?

Tumbo   Please do. (*Exit Jusper. Tumbo, hands in pockets, looks about the room touching this object, then that. Regina enters, followed by Jusper.*)

Regina   Good morning! Have you two met?

Tumbo   No, we haven't, but I am sure you know who I am.

Jusper   Actually I don't.

Tumbo   You must be one of the very few. Ever heard of a Mr. Tumbo?

Jusper   I know the name but . . .

Regina   Don't take him seriously. He is a pain in the neck.

Tumbo   They all are, especially when they wear these red rags of theirs. What is your name?

Jusper   Jusper Wendo.

Tumbo   That is a familiar name. Your prayer was very interesting.

Regina   Does this one pray?

Tumbo   His name was signed against what they called "a student's prayer".

Regina   What was the prayer about?

Jusper   Just a short prayer for our nation. That's all.
We asked God to help us drop our Christian names.

Tumbo   Young man, you had better watch what you
say. If it had half suggested that, you would be behind
bars.

Jusper   But there is nothing wrong with that.
Changing names is item number three in the new
Development Plan isn't it? In fact, Boss himself gave us
a fine example when he substituted his Christian name
with something none of us can pronounce.

Regina   (*hand on mouth*) You! That mouth of yours
will be your undoing. Mr. Tumbo, please don't take him
seriously. He is only a spoilt child.

Jusper   Only a spoilt child, but the worst you can do
to truth is to clothe it in lies. You can't undo it.

Regina   Shut that mouth before someone finds
cause to shut it for you. It isn't as if we have had enough.

Tumbo   Actually, between the three of us, the young
man has a point. We all feel the same but . . . . . but know
better than to shout about it.

Regina   But that name is not difficult to pronounce!?

Jusper   Alright, it may not be difficult to
pronounce, but just what is African about it? Is it the
sound of it or its origin?

Tumbo   A leader needs a mysterious name. A name
that common tongues will bleed pronouncing.

Jusper   A fine preoccupation that one—finding ways
to outwit the common man. It's a shame and it smells.

Tumbo   Do not expect to find refuge in the common
man. You will learn that when you are of age.

Jusper   That is just because our society breeds more
uncommon men than common these days. Our eyes are

forever turned up. Nobody ever looks down. That to me is what that prayer was all about.

Regina   Organising Secretary to the national student's body; just a name for a nobody.

Jusper   I give meaning to that title.

Regina   Ignore him Mr. Tumbo. I understand the visit is on.

Jusper   God help Kafira! The visitor's ghost is all over the place.

Regina   (*seeking to change the topic*) Does any of you care for coffee?

Tumbo   Coffee at this time of day? Come on, we can do better than that. Let's have a cold drink. Does your cousin drink?

Regina   There is no brand of beer he hasn't tasted.

Tumbo   That is the trouble with our students. They simply drink too much. My friend, how much do you drink?

Jusper   I suppose it's as much as you drank off the pocket money you got during your university days.

Tumbo   (*a bit embarrassed*) Actually, I . . . well, I was never there really, but . . . . I mean . . . . I qualified alright but my family was so poor that I decided to sell the scholarship.

Jusper   I had no idea that this kind of thing had a long history.

Tumbo   No, what I do mean is that . . . . I . . . . well . . . . I withdrew . . . . I am of course confusing myself with the language of the bank. They were very poor in those days.

Jusper   The banks were?

Tumbo   Yes, the banks . . . no, I mean my family.

I had to work, but I don't regret it. Education no longer matters these days.

Jusper   You've put your finger on it. The younger generation can only be spectators at most. We'll never have the opportunity to join in that nation-building.

Tumbo   There are opportunities, but they don't come on a plate.

Jusper   The opportunities you talk of can only be described as potential and you know how everlasting these potentialities can be.

Tumbo   You students talk too much. This country needs men of action. If I had depended on empty talk when I came back from abroad two years ago, I would not be owning this block and that other one. You were born alone, and when you die, you will die alone. Why then do you want to ruin your chances by pretending to talk for others? We are here for a season. That is what you students don't understand. You won't be a student for ever, you know. Learn to fight for yourself and then when your presence is felt, you can risk shouting for others.

Jusper   That is the surest way to build a man-eat-man society. Can you justify my release from prison? Can you justify . . .

Regina   I am about to go and make that coffee.

Tumbo   No, please, allow me to . . er . . er . . . Mr. Wendo, can you drive?

Jusper   I never dreamt of that.

Tumbo   Come off it. A Jaguar is the easiest car to drive; especially the new automatic ones. You see, the gears are . . . .

Jusper   What are gears? (*silence*) Send me. I will walk.

Tumbo   Oh, great! (*gives him money*) I take White
Cap, and you?

Jusper   Any beer will do. We students can't afford to
discriminate.

Tumbo   And you?

Jusper   My cousin takes Tusker.

Regina   I don't. Get me a soft drink, you know which.

Tumbo   Surely you can do better than that? Get her
a bottle of red wine.

Regina   No. He knows what I take.

Jusper   How many bottles each?

Regina   Just bring one each, and remember to take
off that thing before you go.

Tumbo   Don't let her limit us. As the saying goes,
money is not the problem; the problem is how to spend
it. (*Jusper picks up a bag from under the bed. He's about to
walk out when Regina stops him.*)

Regina   Jusper!

Jusper   Madam.

Regina   The gown!

Jusper   No, I can't take it off. It will make him angry.

Tumbo   Oh no, I don't get angry that easily.

Jusper   Not you! (*exit*).

Regina   I hope you don't mind him talking that way
to you Mr. Tumbo? It's the way he was brought up.
Besides, I suspect he is a little drunk already.

Tumbo   He's alright. There is something in him,
a kind of finality that I admire. What does he study at
university?

Regina   He is a philosophy student, though he
prefers literature. Sits in here all day long, writing
playlets.

Tumbo   Oh, he may be the very man I want. He writes plays, does he?

Regina   Yes, why?

Tumbo   We need a play. I am sure I told you that they appointed me chairman of the visitor's entertainment committee.

Regina   You did.

Tumbo   We have decided to include a one-act play on our programme. Boss is very keen on the idea. You know his love for the arts, especially theatre. The play will highlight some of our achievements since independence. If your cousin can write one, there is a good potato in it.

Regina   I am sure he will be thrilled.

Tumbo   He better be. You don't come by that kind of money that easily. You see, the whole programme is to cost the Government some quarter of a million shillings. In fact, I had a mind of writing the play myself, but I thought better of it. You see, I am a socialist at heart, so I said to myself: let me extend this opportunity to someone else. I said to myself: "Tumbo, you have not done badly, why don't you lead the pack of them. Show them light, eat and let eat."

Regina   I wish the others felt the same way.

Tumbo   Things will change. Boss is not at all bad at heart. His main problem is that he gets scared far too easily. That is why his advisers are in fact ruling Kafira. That is why he feigns toughness. Mind you he does it so well that his own guards hate his guts, but they do not talk beyond whispers. The worst of the advisers is that cousin of his, Mulili.

Regina   I understand he has been given a large farm

for his services to the nation.

Tumbo   It is true. That is why he retired from the
Army. He now calls himself a farmer. Until people like
him are out, it is dangerous to seem to do things
differently in Kafira. It just proves that there are
questions in your mind.

Regina   Those who know him well say he is not at
all bad except for his short temper.

Tumbo   His main fault lies in making hasty
decisions, and then standing by them; and then he has
this ridiculous weakness for women.

Regina   Now you are talking. If you must know,
that is why I fear to see him personally. I have this funny
feeling that something will go wrong.

Tumbo   No, you must not fear. If you want your
brother released, then you must see him yourself. Of
course I am doing the best I can under the
circumstances. Incidentally, I understand from the
prison warder that Mosese has finally been persuaded
to take part.

Regina   Has he?

Tumbo   He has.

Regina   Thank God! I had feared he would remain
adamant.

Tumbo   It now remains for you to play your cards
right.

Regina   When I told him of my intention to plead
with Boss, he was so furious that he asked me never to
pay him another visit if I talked with Boss.

Tumbo   You shouldn't have told him, you know.
I told you it was to remain secret for the time being.

Regina   But why shouldn't he know? I thought he

would be happy that at least there is some hope.

Tumbo   He should know better than to refuse you making this visit. It is for his own good. Besides I have already made an appointment for you.

Regina   But how could you? Supposing I don't make it?

Tumbo   You'll make it alright. He'll send a driver to pick you up at 2 p.m.

Regina   The day?

Tumbo   Next Saturday.

Regina   I want to come, but something inside me . . .

Tumbo   We can't afford to make him angry at this stage. (*knock at the door*)

Regina   Come in. (*enter Jusper*)

Tumbo   So you see, a block like this one cost me no less than one hundred and fifty thousand shillings. (*looks at Jusper*) You really are a fast walker.

Jusper   I am sorry. (*Drinks are served. Regina takes the remaining ones to the inner rooms.*)

Tumbo   Aaa! God knows I needed that drink. It's a tough job being a top government servant. Aaa! This is a great drink; yet some people say we are not really independent. Let me ask you, would we drink like this if we weren't independent?

Jusper   I suppose not.

Tumbo   The answer if you ask me, is simply No! (*He bursts out laughing and laughs rather too loudly.*) So, what are you hoping to do during your forthcoming vacation?

Jusper   Welcome the visitor.

Tumbo   That will not add an ounce to your weight.

Jusper   In that case I shall simply sit here and vegetate. No one wants to trust us with anything, since we sit on the fence. We are neither children nor adults.

Tumbo   You should do something useful for yourself. Your cousin informs me that you write plays.

Jusper   Yes, just to pass time. To escape for a few moments from reality.

Tumbo   Are any of them published?

Jusper   No one will publish them. They say it is dangerous.

Tumbo   Dangerous?

Jusper   Yes. One publisher simply returned the manuscript and with it one line. It read: 'I am afraid your manuscript is unpublishable under the present circumstances; your truth is too much in the nude.' He wanted me to dress up the truth, give it a little more padding so that only few would recognise it.

Tumbo   What kind of truth was it?

Jusper   It is as if it's a crime to have eyes and ears.

Tumbo   You should consider publishing it abroad.

Jusper   No. I will wait until we are of age. At present nobody wants things put in black and white. You need a little grey and perhaps a blue here and there.

Tumbo   It isn't that clear cut, is it?

Jusper   If you think I lie, ask Soyinka.

Tumbo   Who is Soyinka? Oh . . . I see, the Prime Minister of . . . oh I forget the country.

Jusper   The one I know is only an artist.

Tumbo   Only an artist? Are you sure? That is a politician's name.

Jusper   All sensitive artists are in danger of being branded politicians. To poke your nose in other people's affairs is to be political. A politician these days is anyone who tries to tell people what they already know.

Tumbo   Is it the beer or is that what you actually write about?

Jusper   It may be the beer. The effect is tremendous when you haven't tasted it for months.

Tumbo   What kind of plays do you write then?

Jusper   Absurd. It's the only way to safely get the truth across. Only a few things are in black and white; the rest is darkness.

Tumbo   Just the kind of play we need for the great day. A play that will outline our achievements in black and white and ignore the dark side of the picture. Do you think you can write one for that purpose?

Jusper   What is it in aid of?

Tumbo   It's an item on the entertainment programme. There is good money in it. What achievements would you highlight for example?

Jusper   You can't run short of them. The number of expatriate professionals has steadily increased over the years, signifying the full extent of our potential progress.

Tumbo   Good, I am glad you think in terms of progress. May I assure you now that your prize-winning play will be performed for the visitor?

Jusper   Prize-winning?

Tumbo   Yes. A sum of money has been allocated for a play-writing competition, but there is no point in organizing a competition if we already know what play ought to be produced. You see, my friend, the democratic aspect of this game is that anyone has a right to participate. Now, without wasting any more time, I pronounce you winner of the proposed play-writing competition.

Jusper   (*obviously amused*) Out of the more than

eighty plays submitted, Jusper Wendo's play came first.

Tumbo   You've got it, son. Only make sure that you have the play by tomorrow. News of your having won the competition will be in the papers next week.

Jusper   The other entries have, of course, been returned to their authors.

Tumbo   You are there son, you are there. Now three cheers to the winner. Hip! Hip! Regina!

Regina   (*from kitchen*) Yes, cheers.

Tumbo   Give us a minute. (*enter Regina wiping her hands with the lower edge of her dress*) Regina, it's all settled. Your cousin has won the play-writing competition. That saves the government a lot of money. No need to run up and down looking for one little play.

Regina   But isn't that . . .

Tumbo   Jusper, tell your cousin that life is not a straight line.

Jusper   Regina, life is not a straight line.

Tumbo   Good. Now of the six hundred pounds that was to finance the competition, I give one third to the two of you. The other two thirds will be used to put the records straight. But remember all this is in strict confidence. Your prize money will be sent to you as soon as the results of the competition are made public.

Regina   I still feel that. . .

Tumbo   Jusper, tell your cousin that we are here for only a season.

Jusper   Regina, we are here for only a season.

Tumbo   And who knows, your cousin here may even sit on the dais with the rest of us. Young man, shake my hand. You are a very fortunate student. You can't get that kind of money by digging among books

in that library of yours. No sir, you need a different kind
of this. (*points to his head*)

Jusper How long do you want it?

Tumbo About forty-five minutes, and make sure
the words 'progress' and 'achievement' appear on every
other page. It should be ready before lunch tomorrow.
Regina, may I have a word with you?

Jusper (*removes money from his pocket*) Mr. Tumbo,
your change.

Tumbo Oh, that! Keep change. I know you students
only have money in theory. Bye.

Jusper Bye. (*Exeunt Tumbo and Regina. Wendo, still
holding the money in his hand, moves downstage to remind the
audience of what he holds.*) The fruits of independence. We
get them second-hand. (*fade lights.*)

act two

scene one

A table and four chairs. A water jar and glasses. Kabito is asleep on one of the chairs. Nicodemo walks in and wakes him up.

Nicodemo   Kabito, wake up. Didn't you sleep at all last night?

Kabito   Leave me alone.

Nicodemo   I don't except members of the committee to fall asleep before the meeting even starts. Where are the others?

Kabito   How am I to know?

Nicodemo   Did you get the potato?

Kabito   What potato?

Nicodemo   The university potato. Did your tender go through?

Kabito   Don't remind me of things I would sooner forget. I spent the whole of last night being nice to people, only to lose the tender this morning.

Nicodemo   Whom did they give it to?

Kabito   Who else? The fools gave it to Mulili.

Nicodemo   I knew he would bully them into giving it to him.

Kabito   And as if that is not enough, Tumbo puts him on this committee. I refuse to sit with thieves on the same committee.

Nicodemo   I understand that Tumbo was forced to have him on the committee for security reasons.

Kabito   As far as I am concerned, Mulili is an army drop-out and a second-rate farmer. What does he know about entertaining an important visitor? This is not an agricultural show. If he doesn't get me first, I will get him.

Nicodemo   Report the matter to Boss first.

Kabito   Are you new here? You should know that to report Mulili to Boss is to dig your own grave.

Nicodemo   That is everybody's fear, but someone has to make a start. Take this case of prisoners being asked to act for the visitor: I mean, it's ridiculous. They are now being treated as if they belong to this world. Every time they have rehearsals, I am told they eat bread and butter. It just doesn't make sense.

Kabito   On the contrary, it makes a lot of sense. What effect do you think a few photographs of fat prisoners will have on our foreign investment?

Nicodemo   If that Mosese fellow is pardoned, it will be a personal tragedy for me. I oppose this whole idea of prisoners sharing the dais with the rest of us. (*Tumbo enters with a big file under his armpit.*)

Tumbo   Good morning gentlemen.

Nicodemo }
Kabito   } Good morning.

Tumbo   Just as I expected, Mulili is yet to come.

Kabito   What is he doing on the committee anyway?

Tumbo   You know better than that, Kabito. In any case, that question is not on the agenda. I trust, gentlemen, that you know why you sit on this committee. You were nominated for one reason: your unflinching support for our government. Our aim should be to justify your selection. (*drinks water*) Our task is to prepare and recommend plans for the formal welcome of the visitor. As per circular 02/007/4 B.P., which I am sure you all have, Boss himself stresses the need to

delight the visitor. Remember it is through this visit that
the voice of our negotiators may continue to be heard.

Nicodemo   Excuse me Mr. Tumbo, I think you are
being a little too formal. It isn't as if we are friends here.
(*Nicodemo and Kabito laugh.*)

Kabito   I agree with Nicodemo. Let's drop the
formality until Mulili comes. You see, you only joined
us recently; so perhaps the way things are done here has
escaped your eye. The tree-climber begins from the
bottom, not the top. May we not be told our terms of
service, or are we being good citizens?

Nicodemo   Yes, what size of potato per hour?

Tumbo   You will be paid per day, not per hour.

Nicodemo   How many working days do you think...?

Kabito   Of course it will be necessary for us to meet
everyday until the visitor arrives. In fact, I think it will
be necessary for us to meet after the visit for the purpose
of review.

Nicodemo   You couldn't be more correct. He is a
visitor of great weight, not some flywhisk-waving
sub-headman. And remember also Mr. Chairman that the
potato you get will be directly proportional to the potato
we get. (*enter Mulili almost out of breath*)

Mulili   Gentlemen, I am very sorrowful, but I always
say, better never than late.

Tumbo   What is the excuse this time?

Mulili   (*beaming with happiness*) This time? You see,
yesterday they termination my tender.

Tumbo   Tender, did you say?

Mulili   Yes, my tender for supply of milk to
University. They gives it to unknown small man. So this
morning, I says okay, we see if University authority

know who man be head and neck of Kafira. So I wakes
up, I go to my cousin to explanation him.

Tumbo   You are sure you were with Boss?

Mulili   One God! When I tells him, he take a
automatic direct telephone wire to University. (*acts out
Boss*) Hallo, that is catering University manager? Good,
listen me. What happen to Mr. Mulili tender for supply
milk? What? You knows who speaking? It is me, me
Boss himself, no bloody vice-deputy. Yess, alright
cancel now. Tender Mulili's. (*bursts out laughing*) You see,
first come first saved.

Tumbo   Can anyone ever beat you at this?

Mulili   Not anyone. I am old hand of this. Now it
remain for me to look for who go behind my back to
make them cancel it yesterday. As soon as they tells me,
that man is regret the day he come from stomach.

Tumbo   Alright, back to business. Your lateness, it
seems, is justified.

Mulili   Yes, justice. They wanting to rob me in
sunlight. (*laughs again*)

Tumbo   We are discussing what should be included
in the programme.

Mulili   Oh, I see, thank you. The first thing to me is
. . . . tribalistic dances.

Tumbo   Tribal dances?

Kabito   (*head in arms*) He means traditional dances.

Mulili   Yes traditional tribes and dances. (*Tumbo
takes notes.*)

Nicodemo   Put this down. School children to line up
along Airport Road right up to Government House. We
have enough children in town, don't we?

Mulili   I objection Mr. Chairman. What we do, we

do this: we ask for holiday, then every movable adult to line the road, not only children.

Kabito Forget about children lining the road. This is their final term and most of them will be sitting for their exams. The visitor will understand; after all, it doesn't happen where he comes from. We must guard against one way traffic.

Mulili I objection Mr. Chairman! Children should must see for themself. They are tomorrow leaders you know. And another thing, last year we gives them freedom of primary learning. Put down.

Kabito Good Grief!

Mulili What are you good grief for?

Tumbo Alright; we'll take a vote. Who is against that point? (*confused stares*) Who is for the point? (*more confused stares*) Okay, on the strength of the Chairman's vote, it has been decided that school children will line up along Airport Road to welcome the visitor.

Kabito What about an upcountry visit? He might be interested in seeing for himself the progress we have made in agriculture. He offered us all the technicians for the projects, didn't he?

Tumbo I am afraid that is outside the scope of this committee. We must confine ourselves to the visitor's stay in the city. Any other suggestions?

Nicodemo I still don't understand why we are using prisoners in that play. Prisoners are dangerous people who must not be allowed to mix with the rest of us on the dais.

Kabito The drama department of our National University should be given the responsibility of producing the play.

Tumbo That cannot be. The students are opposed to the nature of this visit. They will not co-operate. They have even sacked their own Organising Secretary for his positive contribution.

Mulili Who do they thinks they are not to co-operate? We pays for their fees, we pays for their luxury food, we give them all necessary, who are they? We should can force them to acting.

Kabito You are the people who choke Kafira. How do you expect to force grown-ups to do a thing they do not believe in? What do you think would be the long term consequences?

Mulili You says that because your son is there, eeh? Say yes!

Kabito That is all you seem to know, commanding people to say, 'yes'. Just what do you take them for? Primary school kids?

Mulili Who you call primary kid? I asks you now, who you call primary kid? This is not first time you calls me that. Tell me now why you . . .

Tumbo Alright Mr. Mulili, I didn't hear him call you. . .

Mulili He do just now. He call me primary. Mr Nicodemo hear him even.

Nicodemo I think we need a break.

Mulili But why he call me primary kid?

Kabito Alright Professor, tell us the day you stepped inside a secondary school classroom.

Mulili You must apology to me this now.

Kabito I will never apologise to the likes of you.

Tumbo Please listen gentlemen. We have a duty to serve our nation. Let us not spoil our image by allowing grudges from the past to take the better of us. Surely we can do better than this. I agree with Nicodemo that we need a break to let off steam. Now, how long shall we have it?

Nicodemo   Three hours should be enough.

Tumbo   Three hours is a long time to let off steam. Alright let's take one hour's break. Please remember to come back on time.

Kabito   I hope he has heard it. (*He glares briefly at Mulili, then strides off. Mulili shouts after him.*)

Mulili   You plays with fire you goat!
(*fade lights*)

scene two

Outside Boss's Palace. Boss sits in an arm chair. He holds a small mirror which he uses as he pulls out grey hairs from his head.

Boss   Grey hair signifies wisdom, but it is a sad reminder. A kind of constant pointer to the passing of time. A leader should not grow grey: people begin to lose confidence in you. (*He is about to remove a grey hair when Mulili walks in*) Hey you, I hate people who move quietly—do you hear? Next time, let some noise accompany your movement.

Mulili   Yes cousin; but why you sits out without body-guard?

Boss   Why have you come? Another tender problem, is it?

Mulili   No, no tender problem. They all fears when you spoken to them on the telephone box.

Boss   Why have you left the meeting then?

Mulili   Honest to God, I don't know how to begins. I have no tongue to talk.

Boss   Come on, get on with it.

Mulili   Boss, you are cousin and I tells you this. Things have spoil. Don't trust anybody, not even me.

Boss   You talk straight or go back to the meeting. I put you on the committee for obvious reasons and I expect you to report directly to me if something should seem to be going wrong. What is the matter?

Mulili   I can't believe it even now. It is a big ugly matter I tells you. Do you know Kabito? He be like Jere.

Boss   I know many Kabitos.

Mulili   I am saying the one on the entertain committee.

Boss   What about him?

Mulili   That one, he be a green grass in the snake.

Boss   Watch what you say. Kabito is one of my most loyal subjects.

Mulili   Oho! That what you thinks. You thinks I just leave meeting for little reason? He colour your name in blood in front of whole committee. You see, in first place, he come to meeting full of alcoholism.

Boss   Drunk, is he?

Mulili   Completely finished. He shout to everybody and say you rob him milk tender.

Boss   He can't have possibly said that.

Mulili   One God in heaven! He say you ruins the economic of Kafira. That you hides million in foreign country.

Boss   Who? Kabito?

Mulili   A green grass in the snake, I tells you.

Boss   I keep money in foreign lands? Who gave him the information? (*grabs Mulili*) Just how much does Kabito know about my private life? No, perhaps he was only joking. A kind of trick to lure the others into speaking their mind.

Mulili   Joking? Boss you jokes yourself. That man even say you try to get that Regina by force.

Boss   Tumbo must have a hand in this.

Mulili   No. Tumbo himself tell him: "Hey, Kabito, that is high slandering," but Kabito just shout louder. It was alcoholism.

Boss   That is no excuse. He must be the one who poisoned Mercedes's mind. That woman has never been so rude to me before. Who told her about that girl?

Mulili   I can't know. But I suspects Kabito.

Boss   When a man plays with fire, he gets burned.
He will serve as an example to others that may have hot
mouths like him.

Mulili   I looked at him and said to myself: "This
man is fit to go mental."

Boss   Go get him. Take two guards with you and
bring him to me. No, wait a minute. I shall not set my
eyes upon him. Mulili!

Mulili   Cousin!?

Boss   Come here. I shall not allow small people to
sow seeds of discord among the people. You know what
must be done?

Mulili   I am old hand at everything.

Boss   Come report to me that he is silent.

Mulili   That be small. You remembers that old
couple . . . ?

Boss   (*shouting*) Clear out of my sight and get on with
it. (*exit Mulili*)

(*fade lights*)

scene three

Same as Act Two, Scene One, except for the glasses and the jar which are missing.

Jusper   I don't want you to feel I am betraying you. It's just that I can't go on after what has happened. Regina thinks I shouldn't, and I agree with her.

Tumbo   I warn you that it's too dangerous. It is sabotage. You go off and think about it. We can't do without you at this crucial stage. I know how Regina must feel, but then we can't let our emotions overcome reason.

Jusper   She had to escape by jumping out of a ten-foot high window.

Tumbo   It's a great shame.

Jusper   I can't believe it. Imagine locking up his wife for complaining about the incident.

Tumbo   So many things are happening in Kafira that I guess we are about to experience some major change. I hope Mosese does not hear of the incident.

Jusper   I hope so too, otherwise this whole programme will have to be scrapped.

Tumbo   Pass my apologies to Regina. God, she must take me for a devil!

Jusper   She will never forgive you.

Tumbo   I swear to God that I recommended it in good faith. Maybe I should try to see her personally.

Jusper   That might help.

Tumbo   Go get the new rehearsal schedule, and remember: one faulty step, and your university studies could come to an abrupt end. Already you have lost more than a year.

Jusper I don't mind losing another if that is what it means to stand for truth and justice.

Tumbo If you knew what has happened to one of us on the committee, I am sure you would postpone your eagerness to stand by truth and justice. (*pause*) I hope to see you in two hours' time.

Jusper I will come, but I do not guarantee to sit on the truth as it is. I feel we have done wrong . . .

Tumbo Sshh! See you. (*Exit Jusper as Nicodemo enters. Silence.*)

Nicodemo So you have also heard?!

Tumbo I can't believe it. It's beyond talk.

Nicodemo But you believe it was an accident?

Tumbo What does it matter what I believe? There are millions of stories on our lips. Somehow, I felt it coming. Kabito should have known better than to confront him that directly.

Nicodemo I, too, sensed that something would go wrong after that quarrel. Do you think we should keep quiet about the quarrel?

Tumbo We have no choice. Like caged animals, we move, but only inside the cage. It has become infectious —this desire to eliminate others. Here he comes. Remember we know nothing. (*enter Mulili*)

Mulili Oh, gentlemen, this world is upside down. I can't believes it myself. It is worst news.

Tumbo What?

Mulili Our friend Kabito. He get fatal accident during break.

Nicodemo You can't be serious! Fatal did you say?

Mulili It is very sad and very sad. He is dead. You

see, people come and report accident and I run to spot.
Oh, who did me see but Kabito! The ambulance have
takes the body away.

Tumbo   Just what could have happened?

Mulili   Accident . . . . Driving under influential
alcohol.

Nicodemo   Just how drunk can one get in the space
of one hour?

Mulili   I also ask that, then people say his breath
smelled full of spirits. The hard stuff!

Nicodemo   His breath, did you say?

Mulili   Who said breath? I said his body smelled
whiskies.

Tumbo   Is Boss aware of it?

Mulili   Boss is with tears in his eyes. He says that
one road is immediately to be Kabito Road.

Tumbo   What is to be done now?

Nicodemo   I suppose we call off the meeting?

Mulili   Yes, meeting off.

Tumbo   I will let you know when the next meeting
will be. Let us observe one minute's silence in honour
of the departed. . . . Thank you.

Nicodemo   Will this day be counted? (*Tumbo stares
at Nicodemo. Nicodemo stares at Mulili.*)
(*Lights fade.*)

scene four

Stage is set for the final rehearsal of the visitor's play. Jusper, who carries bits of costume, props and a script, now begins to put the final touches to the stage. Tumbo soon joins him.

Tumbo   Have they set it right?

Jusper   It will do.

Tumbo   Of course there will be other additions like the red carpet, and the other decorations.

Jusper   It will do. In such circumstances, almost anything will. Mind you, we have to improvise with the resources at hand. After all we are only a developing country.

Tumbo   We can't take any chances; he is in such an unpredictable mood that he has even locked up his own wife in the Palace cell. He nearly slapped. . . . I mean he was very cross with me when I told him we don't have all the props.

Jusper   I am determined that nothing should go wrong.

Tumbo   The future of six hundred prisoners depends on it. And that includes Mosese. By the way, did he co-operate fully during last night's rehearsal?

Jusper   He was at his best. He knew all the lines and moves and went through them as if he had lived with them all his life.

Tumbo   You know, I have not had the chance to go through the script.

Jusper   But then you have been busy.

Tumbo   That is no excuse. If he should ask for the story of the play, I will point at you and say, "Your Excellency, the author of the play is better qualified to give that information." I trust you will face him and answer that question with precision.

Jusper   I will try.

Tumbo   It is too late to say you will try. You will do it.

Jusper   Why do you appear nervous?

Tumbo   Boy, you still don't understand the principles of survival. When he loses his temper, he can hardly tell a human being from a rat. The man is an animal, I tell you, and this is one of his bad months if you believe in astrology.

Jusper   We shall make a permanent impression, I am sure. That will help me to convince my fellow students, who threw me out, that it is not by isolation that problems are solved. They sacked me, said I was going round the bend again, called me a traitor and betrayer of their cause. If this play is a success, I will have demonstrated that determination is greater in worth than numbers.

Tumbo   Do you intend to lead them afterwards?

Jusper   If there is an afterwards, it will sort itself out. We have no future until we see it in the past. That is the only time we may know we once had a future. Mosese once had a future, until he came to my brother's funeral.

Tumbo   Was he your real brother?

Jusper   Same father, same mother, and he made me kill, but they set me free. Knew I was no longer dangerous, but what about Mosese?

Tumbo   He should make maximum use of what luck brings his way. Why did you not tell me these things before?

Jusper   What would you have done? I am still the same.

Tumbo I know, but I am worried. I don't think Boss knows it's your play we are performing. We have to keep it secret. All he knows is that you are a student.

Jusper Why are you worried?

Tumbo Because I know I like you. I also know that the day of a man's death is not written on his forehead. Kabito is a case in point. You will have to talk less. Your blood is well known.

Jusper That means that the release of a few prisoners will not change Kafira. The sun will still rise in the east and set in the west.

Tumbo The image of Kafira will be different in the eyes of the world.

Jusper We only help to obscure the true picture. The release of a few prisoners is, in fact, a positive distortion of the picture.

Tumbo You want them out, don't you?

Jusper Yes, but I do not wish to see them come from one prison only to enter another. (*Boss takes them by surprise.*)

Boss Everything in place?

Tumbo Yes, Your Excellency.

Boss Drop the formality. We are all actors here. Boy, did you know I was once a good actor?

Jusper We all know it, sir.

Boss Good. Only they almost always gave me bad roles. In four out of five cases, I had to die for little mistakes that were not my own. Do you still call that tragic?

Jusper I would say it's sacrifice. A kind of death for a future. The sort of role Christ played.

Boss Death for a future? Yes, that is absolutely

necessary. Are you the author of the play?

Jusper   We could say so, but friends helped me alter it.

Boss   Good, that is positive unity. I understand you study at the University?

Jusper   Yes, sir.

Boss   Represent the intellectuals well. (*seriously*) Some of the reports I get from there are simply disgusting. Who made you students spokesmen of truth and justice? What do you know about justice?

Jusper   Nothing, Your Excellency.

Boss   Completely nothing. Take the second last time, for instance: what was it they were protesting against? Speak out! There will be no victimisation.

Jusper   The influx of expatriate personnel into the country.

Boss   Now, listen to that. Do they want to walk before they can crawl? When you go back, tell their leaders that it is my duty to decide on the magnitude of Kafira's africanisation programme. They have no right to chant about it; and if they do, the result will always be the same. What do you think they gained by that demonstration?

Jusper   Nothing, sir.

Boss   Completely nothing. A dead student leader and a senior lecturer in prison . . . . . no, no, the lecturer went in for a different offence. Not so?

Tumbo   (*glad to join in*) Completely.

Boss   In a way, it was very sad. They should have known my arms are long. My eyes see far, and my ears are the sharpest on the continent. Am I wrong?

Tumbo   (*still nervous*) Yes, sir.

Boss Wrong?

Tumbo Who, you sir? No! Never!

Boss No one who shouts at me ever gets what they want. You saw what happened the last time, didn't you?

Jusper Yes, Your Excellency.

Boss Because they shouted against the appointments, five of which were my own personal appointments, I deliberately sent in an order for three hundred more expatriate personnel, just to put them in their place.

Tumbo Most of them lack understanding. They are too young.

Boss Precisely, they just don't reason like leaders of tomorrow. I understand they even wanted to demonstrate against the visit. I warn them that I will not tolerate such behaviour in Kafira. Do you hear?

Jusper Yes, sir.

Boss Where are the others.

Tumbo Dressing up, sir.

Boss Go inside and call all the staff. We need an audience.

(*exit Tumbo*)

I hope it's a good play. What is it called?

Jusper "Betrayal in the City."

Boss Betrayal in the City? That's a curious title. What is it all about?

Jusper Army cadet.

Boss Army cadet? That should be interesting. The visitor himself was in the army for seven years before he joined active politics. What does the cadet do?

Jusper The main drama is built around what he doesn't do, or rather around what is done for him. In the first place, he is promoted to the rank of captain within six months of his enrolment . . .

Boss   Hmm, very hard working.

Jusper   Because he doesn't quite know how to handle a gun, he accidentally shoots his colleague during a pass-out parade.

Boss   That is manslaughter.

Jusper   The climax is reached when it is discovered that he is not, in fact, a relative of the army commander as had been thought.

Boss   It sounds very interesting. Is it a commedy or a tragedy?

Jusper   It is neither, but it could be both.

Boss   But someone dies?

Jusper   It is possible to have a death that is not tragic.

Boss   Very clever. The first time I have heard sense spoken by a student. (*enter Mulili and a few Palace staff*) Come for the final rehearsal?

Mulili   Yes, Your Excellent. I say to myself: go and be with cousin as he see the final one.

Boss   Good, make yourself comfortable.
(*enter Tumbo, Askari and more Palace staff*)

Tumbo   Sir, I understand that one of the actors—the one who was to have played the chief of staff—is not well.

Boss   What is the matter with him?

Askari   Stomach troubles, Your Excellency. The doctor has recommended rest for him.

Boss   The affairs of state shall not be halted just because of the stomach troubles of one prisoner. I must see the full-dress rehearsal.

Jusper Perhaps we should get someone to read his part for the moment sir; it will save time.

Boss Alright then, Tumbo will read it. (*Mulili hails the idea.*) Were you ever an actor?

Tumbo No sir.

Boss (*jokingly*) Then how did you become a big man? (*general response to His Excellency's joke*)

Mulili If he could not, then I should read for the part.

Boss Alright; we shouldn't waste time. I will stand in for him for the moment. Give me the script. Thank you. Where am I to stand?

Jusper You are to sit on that chair, Sir. (*Boss goes to the chair as Mosese and Jere are brought in hand-cuffed. They are in their acting costumes.*)

Boss Are they to act like that? Untie their hands! (*Askari unties them*).

Jusper (*nervously*) Sir, what about the props?

Tumbo The carpenter we asked to make guns has not yet made them.

Boss (*angrily*) I will not have this. I hate last minute strugglers. I want to see you with all the props first thing tomorrow morning, okay?

Tumbo Okay, Sir.

Boss Are the props that vital to this rehearsal?

Tumbo No Your. . .

Jusper Very vital Your Excellency; we need them for the prologue.

Boss Guards!

Guards Sir!

Boss Bring your guns forward and put them. . .

Jusper Here sir. (*Three guards bring their guns foward.*)

Boss   Put them there.

Jusper   His Excellency has kindly agreed to read the part of the chief of staff. Remember the prologue is fast and should only last seven minutes. Ready, let's go. (*Mosese and Jere argue bitterly.*)

Mosese   I can prove it to you now that a .32 automatic is shorter than a .28.

Jere   You surprise me. The two guns are equal.

Mosese   Have you measured? You have only been here six months. How much do you think you can teach us about guns? (*Boss laughs and Mulili joins him.*)

Jere   You lack respect for your seniors. Who gave you permission to argue with me?

Mosese   I am sorry, Captain. (*He salutes, Boss laughs.*)

Jere   That's better. Now, the captain says the two guns are equal: do you agree?

Mosese   I agree sir, but may we see the chief of staff for confirmation.

Jere   You should know better than that. The chief of staff will sooner agree with his captain than listen to a mere lieutenant. Come on then. (*They move to where Boss now sits and mime knocking at the door. Being busy, he will continue to work until after the third knock.*)

Boss   Step in. (*They step in cautiously and salute.*) Yes, what can I do for you?

Mosese   Sir, we have come to enquire whether a .32 automatic is equal to a .28.

Boss   That's very vague. Even you, Captain?

Jere   He won't believe me, Sir.

Boss   Alright, you show me a .32 from those guns, and you captain will show me a .28. (*Mosese and Jere go for the guns. Jusper is over-excited.*)

Jusper   I can't believe it! I can't believe that we have done it on the off-chance!

Boss   I do not see those lines in the script.

Jere   (*pointing his gun at Boss*) No, Your Excellency, such lines are never scripted.

Jusper   I can't believe we've done it. Shoot now! Shoot now!

Boss   Guards, what do. . . ?

Jere   You have no guards, Your Excellency. Remain seated or I'll shoot. People, do not fear. Remain calm, all is well. (*Mulili tries to sneak away.*)

Mosese   Remain seated Mister Mulili.

Mulili   I go for short call.

Mosese   I said, sit down. (*He sits.*)

Jusper   You waste time, pin him down. I said, pin him down. Alright, let me do it. Squad, attention! Aim, one, two, three, two, one tututututu!!!!!!!!! Squad, at ease! (*to Mulili*) Hey, sergeant! Why so sad, eeh? He your cousin or something? ·

Mulili   Oh, no, no, is never!

Jusper   We'll put him in a government coffin. I will design it myself. (*He begins to stride off but is stopped by Mosese.*)

Mosese   Jusper, where are you off to?

Jusper   (*in a sad trembling voice*) To design the coffin.

Mosese   No. Remain where you are. (*to Boss*) See what you have done to him? He alone would justify your death a thousand times, yet you are still alive. Tell me why?

Boss   I do not know why.

Jere   I will show you why. Mulili, come towards me. (*Mulili obeys.*) This man is your cousin.

Mulili   He is only distant cousin, that is all.

Jere   Give me one good reason why he should not be killed.

Mulili   No reason. You can kill.

Jere   Do you agree that he should be got rid of?

Mulili   *Kabisa!* One, he take everything in his hand. Two, he spoil the economic of Kafira. Three, he rule too long. Change is like rest. Four, he kill Kabito.

Boss   Am I hearing right? Mulili? (*to Jere*) Shoot me. Spare me this betrayal. Shoot me!

Jere   No, Your Excellency, we shall not shoot you. Kafira needs each one of us, you included.

Boss   You mean you will not kill me?

Jere   No. What do we stand to gain by your death? Nothing. Our wish was not to swim in human blood, but to provide a mirror for Kafira. A mirror that will reflect the real faces of Kafira's front men. But it is not enough to provide only a mirror. No. We must learn to sacrifice ourselves for a better future. A future where these events that now take place need not be repeated.

Mosese   A future where men like him need not be members of our society. (*to Tumbo*) But we thank you; it was largely through your inefficiency that we have achieved this. So go, depart from our midst. (*Tumbo hesitates, then speaks.*)

Tumbo   I am truly sorry, but I am not entirely to blame. I was trained, but given the wrong job. Once again I am sorry. (*He hesitates, then exits.*)

Jere   We have sacrificed, but it seems we must continue. Look at him. (*pointing to Jusper*) Is he not sacrifice enough? Your Excellency, I now offer myself. Here, shoot me. (*gives him the gun*)

Boss   No. I cannot. I have no reason to.

Jusper   Give it to me! I will sacrifice him! Give it to me!

Mosese   Jusper, stop where you are.

Jusper   Give it to me! (*Boss hands over the gun to Jusper. The latter stares at the weapon unbelievingly. Slowly he turns and surveys the people with his eyes. Finally, the eyes are fixed on Mulili. Now Jusper stands at attention.*) Squad, attention! Aim! (*He aims.*)

Mulili   (*indicating Boss*) Not me. It him!

Jusper   Fire! (*He shoots and Mulili's body slowly falls; now Jusper turns and surveys the people with his eyes once more.*) I did it for Kafira. I did it for all of you people.

(*Jere slowly walks towards Mulili's body. He picks a small particle of soil and lets it drop through his fingers as he speaks.*)

Jere   Dust to dust, ash to ash. (*Slowly everyone freezes into the shape of trees. The picture on stage should be identical to that of the grave-side scene. Mulili's body taking the place of the grave. Birds, insects, frogs, etc. are singing. A drum beats, stops, beats again and stops. In the distance a male voice laments and becomes louder as the man nears the grave. Suddenly all is quiet, then we hear strange ghostly music. Doga's ghost enters, immediately trailed by Nina's. They both go through their movement of the beginning of the first scene, except that now they are ghosts.*)

Doga   Nina, stop where you are! What sort of mother are you? For years you have wept. Do you now fear to set your eyes on this evil? (*He points at Mulili's body and freezes in this position. Nina freezes too. Slowly lights fade.*)

SLOW CURTAIN

LaVergne, TN USA
28 July 2010
191183LV00001B/33/P